perspectives
ON DESIGN
WESTERN CANADA

creative ideas shared by
leading design professionals

Published by

PANACHE
P A N A C H E   P A R T N E R S

Panache Partners, LLC
1424 Gables Court
Plano, TX 75075
469.246.6060
Fax: 469.246.6062
www.panache.com

Publishers: Brian G. Carabet and John A. Shand

Printed in Malaysia

Distributed by Independent Publishers Group
800.888.4741

PUBLISHER'S DATA

Perspectives on Design Western Canada

Library of Congress Control Number: 2011929216

ISBN 13: 978-0-9832398-1-9
ISBN 10: 0-983239-81-9

First Printing 2012

10 9 8 7 6 5 4 3 2 1

Right: Sublime Interiors, page 163

Previous Page: Su Casa Design, page 83

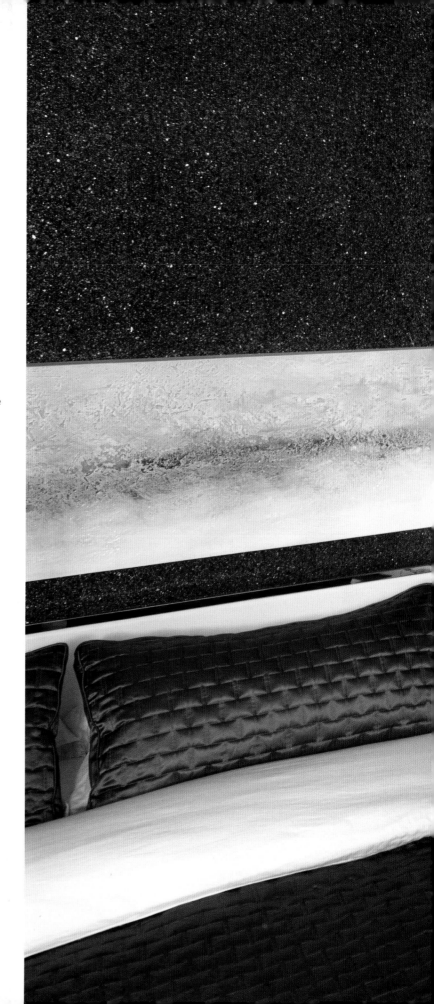

perspectives
ON DESIGN
WESTERN CANADA

South Fraser Stairs, page 137

introduction

Relkie Art Glass, page 201

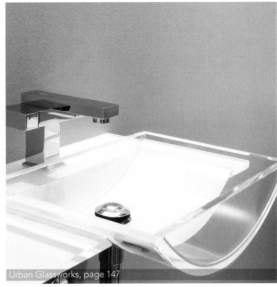

Urban Glassworks, page 147

Creating the spaces in which we live and achieving the beauty we desire can be a daunting quest—a quest that is as diverse as each of our unique personalities. For some, it may be a serene, infinity-edge saltwater pool in the backyard; for others it may be an opulent marble entryway with bronze insets imported from Italy. Aspiring chefs may find a kitchen boasting the finest in technology their true sanctuary.

Perspectives on Design Western Canada is a pictorial journey from conceptualizing your dream home to putting together the finishing touches to creating an outdoor oasis. Alongside the phenomenal photography, you will have a rare insight to how these tastemakers achieve such works of art and be inspired by their personal perspectives on design.

Within these pages, the state's finest artisans will share their wisdom, experience, and talent. It is the collaboration between these visionaries and the outstanding pride and craftsmanship of the products showcased that together achieve the remarkable. Learn from leaders in the industry about the aesthetics of a finely crafted sofa, how appropriate lighting can dramatically change the appearance of a room, or what is necessary to create a state-of-the-art home theater.

Whether your dream is to have a new home or one that has been redesigned to suit your lifestyle, *Perspectives on Design Western Canada* will be both an enjoyable journey and a source of motivation.

concept + structure

elements of structure

contents

elements of design

living the elements

FWC Architecture & Urban Design, page 33

Michael Trayler Designs, page 157

"Every project is like a journey, and the entire process should be enjoyed and savored."

—Tom Bakker

Jake James, page 125

Houston Landscapes, page 189

Burj Enterprises, page 23

FWC Architecture & Urban Design, page 33

concept + structure

Most homeowners are more than familiar with the genres of architecture, construction, and interior design, but only when they embark on the adventure of having their own custom residence created do they fully understand and appreciate the purpose and value of construction management. Artisan Construction and its team of seasoned experts are more than builders; they are communicators who understand the nuances of what it takes to bring complex, award-winning projects to fruition.

The company is the product of Brent Repin's early experiences as an artisan; everywhere he looked, he envisioned better, smarter, more efficient ways of approaching and accomplishing projects. Inspired to take his ideas to a new level, he and his brother Darren founded their own firm, and nearly two decades later they are still some of the youngest professionals in the industry doing the most sought-after projects. With high-profile projects, nothing is off the shelf. Though complete customization requires more time and energy, the Repins and their team don't mind one bit, because attention to every detail is precisely what makes their homes memorable.

"Creating a new home can be an exciting experience, so people are understandably anxious to jump right into the construction phase. That's when we recommend spending just a little bit more time firming up all of the details to ensure that the initial vision is fully realized."

—Brent Repin

ARTISAN CONSTRUCTION

"Being able to transform unpleasant or unusable spaces into innovative focal points is the beauty of construction."

—Darren Repin

ABOVE: The second-story addition includes a master suite that we integrated into one space to form a loft-like feel. Large pieces with clean, simple lines give an uncluttered visual strength, and the layout and material selection allow for views of the water.

FACING PAGE: Native slate, fir, and cedar are incorporated throughout the home's common spaces for a warm West Coast contemporary feel. The kitchen features three different types of countertops: cedar, naturally compressed stone, and resin that mimics beach glass. The resin panel is translucent when underlit, but with the light off it becomes opaque—a very interactive and artful addition.

PREVIOUS PAGES: While revitalizing a decaying beach house into a contemporary residence, we added a second floor and more than 2,000 square feet of decking. Significant structural and geotechnical engineering was required to support the extra weight. We constructed the decks with both functionality and beauty in mind, using elements such as glass railings to seamlessly merge the property with the ocean. The lines of the decking offer striking angularity and visual rhythm, while other details like the sandblasted artglass entry doors exude sophistication and softness.
Photographs by Big Picture Communications

TOP & MIDDLE: Instead of constructing rooms first and then finding suitable décor, we began with existing artwork, furniture, and lighting and created a château-like setting to fit. A large master suite and family room were incorporated on the second level, while the main floor was entirely redesigned to be more family oriented.

BOTTOM: We used a covered patio with a gas fireplace to fade the boundaries between the indoor and outdoor, making the space a natural extension of the living room.

FACING PAGE TOP: A mirrored wall and transparent chandelier not only lend a sense of spaciousness but also whisper of modernism.

FACING PAGE BOTTOM: We turned a previously specified rec room into a media room for a sports and movie enthusiast. The design maintains a refined European feel while incorporating modern amenities. Extensive use of coffers, wainscoting, and arches provides continuity throughout the home.
Photographs by Multivista

"Outstanding communication and collaboration between all parties are essential to successful, timeless projects."

—Brent Repin

RIGHT & FACING PAGE: The home's location in one of Vancouver's exclusive heritage neighborhoods required every decision to accommodate the city's requirements while preserving the architectural character. Extended gable soffits enhance the Tudor style, and half-timbering gives the home a more vertical look. We transformed the rear porch into an outdoor lounge replete with two skylights, winter climate control, and a view of the beautifully landscaped grounds.

Photographs by Big Picture Communications

"Most people have good design sense; they just need a team of professionals to help refine it."

—Darren Repin

ABOVE: We created a multimedia and wellness center with an open floorplan and movable partitions. The indoor Zen garden enjoys natural light thanks to the skylights created by the upper-level outdoor patio's glass floor panels.

FACING PAGE TOP: The foyer immediately introduces a main focus of the home: commissioned art. Crystal pendant lighting, a Martha Sturdy wall sculpture, and area rugs resonate with the exclusive neighborhood and the residents' contemporary lifestyle.

FACING PAGE BOTTOM: The living room's tone-on-tone scheme is punctuated by Asian-inspired floral motifs and lush textures. Above the flush-mount gas fireplace, we installed a theater-grade television that transforms into a mirror when not in use. Electronic draperies allow the homeowners to easily and quickly change the setting to establish different moods.
Photographs by Big Picture Communications

Jeff Burdett grew up working at his father's construction company, where he learned about the world of building from the inside out. Throughout his career, he has worked as a set carpenter for the movie industry, in addition to building custom homes in Japan. Now as president of Burj Enterprises, a recognized builder of high-end residential, commercial, and industrial projects throughout southwestern British Columbia, Jeff uses his expertise to integrate Canada's naturally beautiful environment into high-end custom residences.

With a team of more than 50 employees, Burj Enterprises focuses on modern design with a timeless quality. By working collaboratively with architects and homeowners, Jeff and his team build one-of-a-kind residences that brim with sophisticated details.

"There's a little bit of me in every house. When I build a house, I feel that house belongs to me. I may never stay there, but it's one of my houses."

—Jeff Burdett

BURJ ENTERPRISES

"Modern designs featuring open spaces allow residents to relax and congregate casually and effortlessly."

—Jeff Burdett

LEFT: A full skylight crowns the hallway of the main entrance, bringing natural light into the home. The clear fir doors capitalize on the modern feel with their horizontal lines.

FACING PAGE TOP: To meet the needs of a large family, the open kitchen was designed with lots of working space. Stainless steel appliances and European-steamed beech cabinets add to the space's clean design, while the bar's granite countertop drops to the floor, creating a waterfall effect.

FACING PAGE BOTTOM: The clear tongue and groove cedar ceiling continues to the outside in order to further incorporate nature into the master bedroom. Expansive windows feature breathtaking views of Alta Lake.

PREVIOUS PAGES: A 3,000-square-foot home on Alta Lake serves as a family gathering space for holidays and weekends. The exterior features post-and-beam construction with cedar lap siding, while the home's low profile perfectly blends with the site's elevation.
Photographs by Jason Matthew Henderson

"Details separate a good home from a great home."

—Jeff Burdett

LEFT: A stainless steel mantel coupled with artwork by Martha Sturdy serves as the focal point of the living area, while a built-in storage cabinet made of fir houses a stereo system and a variety of board games. The floating staircase features pre-cast concrete treads that were stained to match the floor's tile.
Photograph by Jason Matthew Henderson

ABOVE: The curved glass railing of the second floor protects the view of the Whistler Blackcomb ski resort. A spacious veranda allows residents to enjoy a hot cup of cocoa as they breathe in the mountain air.

FACING PAGE: A waterfront home on Green Lake incorporates an abundance of glass in order to take advantage of the site's views. A hot tub with a waterfall feature is tucked between the two copper posts on the first floor to further enhance the outdoor experience, while steps made of Petra fan out to the lake.
Photographs by Peter Powles

LEFT: The exterior of the front of the home features a curved wall constructed of basalt stone. While it offers a pleasing aesthetic, the wall also reflects sound from the nearby road so the residents are not disturbed.

FACING PAGE TOP: A limestone fireplace surrounded by horizontal bamboo detailing presents a clean look in the living area. Nine-inch custom-cut oak floors further warm the space. A pond sits outside the window reminding guests that they are enveloped in nature.

FACING PAGE BOTTOM: A modern interpretation of post-and-beam construction accentuates the living room. Accented with wenge wood, the limestone floor adds an interesting detail to the space that is echoed on the front door.
Photographs by Peter Powles

Fook Weng Chan draws inspiration from being challenged. With that in mind, many of his designs can be found on the edge of a cliff or on the top of a mountain, as Fook Weng looks at what most consider impossible sites and sees opportunity. The end results are homes that seamlessly communicate and respond to their environment, while translating the interests and personalities of their owners. Over the years, his work has been described as "crafted contemporary," "romantic modern," and even "spiritual."

Before designing a home, Fook Weng diligently studies the requirements and constraints of the site. Often, this means living with the owner to fully understand how the homeowners live and relate to each other or camping on the site for a few days, which allows him to appreciate its nuances. Many times the information he gleans remains hidden in his subconscious until pencil hits paper.

Prior to starting his own firm in 1995, he was the project architect for a diverse range of structures, including houses, clubhouses, a courthouse, resorts, university buildings, and ceremonial projects. His broad experience allows him to bring a fresh perspective to each project. In addition, limiting the number of projects he takes on enables Fook Weng to closely work with owners and builders to create unique homes that develop their soul over time.

"With every house we try to capture not only the essence of the site but also the essence of the owner."

—Fook Weng Chan

FWC Architecture & Urban Design

"An architect should attempt to fully understand the site and the dynamics of the people who will live there."

—Fook Weng Chan

TOP & MIDDLE: The layout of a home on Orcas Island revolves around the summit of the second tallest mountain on the island. The design unfolds an orchestrated sequence of views that cumulatively tell a story about the site. The two wings of the house are pressed against the summit's tallest rock face, together creating a central garden courtyard. At the homeowner's request, one wing is on axis with Mount Baker, the other oriented to maximize commanding views of the Pacific Northwest Coast. The coziness of the living room, with the courtyard on one edge and the dramatic views of the Salish Sea on the other, is further enhanced with interior furnishings by S.R. Hughes of Tulsa, Oklahoma.
Photographs by Chris Crevier

BOTTOM: The guest suite leads out to a private lavender-edged terrace and overlooks the solar-tube-heated sunken hot tub. The simple design of custom light grilles that have been integrated into the structural columns echoes the architectural vocabulary found throughout the home.
Photograph by Chris Crevier

FACING PAGE: In a Vancouver home, the kitchen is slightly raised above the living and dining room. I jokingly refer to it as "command central" because the mother can easily supervise her children in the living room from this point. Douglas fir post-and-beam construction allows views to be maximized and suggests division of spaces within the great room. Fir cabinetry accented with maple trim adds warmth to the space. A sunken courtyard featuring the soothing sound of gently rushing water against a backdrop of local basalt stone on the high side of the lot provides a focus on axis with the circulation spine in the house. It also admits natural light to the lower levels of the house and allows cross-ventilation.
Photographs by Peter Powles

PREVIOUS PAGES: Designed for a tight, urban, waterfront lot—79 feet wide by 115 feet deep with a 42-foot slope—the 7,000-square-foot home spans three levels. The site offers one particular vista that was extraordinary, so a plan was developed that would allow most of the rooms of the house to be skewed to face that vista. The atrium space of the waterfront home vertically links its three levels, including the entry foyer. A continuous band of skylights provides natural illumination all the way to the basement, even on the greyest winter days.
Photographs by Peter Powles

"Rural sites often have strong settings, views, and topography to respond to. With urban sites, this is not always the case, so a setting must be created for the home. In both scenarios, we find success when there is an effective dialogue between the interior and exterior."

—Fook Weng Chan

ABOVE: A renovation to a traditional urban house involved removing various walls. We figured out where the owners would spend most of their time as a family and reallocated the space of the house. An example of that is the tearoom, which exudes a contemporary feel with a mixture of woods and fiber and a play of translucency versus opacity and smooth versus textured materials.

ABOVE RIGHT: I frequently design furniture and fittings for homes. The custom coffee table in the living area relates back to the design aesthetic of the house.

FACING PAGE: When the owner and I first visited this site, we had to climb onto the knoll with a nylon rope left by the surveyors because it was so steep and rocky. After studying the lot, a home with a sweeping curve that offers breathtaking panoramic views of Howe Sound was conceived. A spa on the bottom floor incorporates native bedrock. The home was one of 27 around the world selected for a primary feature on Discovery Network's "Amazing Vacation Homes."

Photographs by Peter Powles

"A house should never be seen or designed in isolation. Considering the house in relation to its physical context and designing the master plan for site development helps imbue the project with a 'spirit of place.'"

—Fook Weng Chan

TOP LEFT: The foyer of a home overlooking Howe Sound on Bowen Island features custom ceramic work by the owner as well as local timber and granite stone. Local materials and local artisans are used whenever possible—sometimes in unexpected ways. For instance, the roofer made the copper light fixtures.

LEFT: The home sits on the edge of a ragged cliff overlooking Howe Sound. A "campus" of pavilions was created. Each is situated on the lot to offer the best view from its perch. A series of bridges and circulation spines connects the pavilions.

FACING PAGE: A courtyard in the center of the pavilions becomes the focus of the assemblage of forms, blurring the distinction between inside and out. The use of recycled timbers from an old warehouse building further helps blend the design with the forested environment.
Photographs by Peter Powles

ABOVE: A modern staircase in a house at Green Lake in Whistler offers a clean mix of glass, stone, and wood as it leads to the basement. Buried on the high side of the lot, the basement features an open view to the lake.

ABOVE RIGHT: The exterior and landscaping of the home feature a series of "S" curves that takes inspiration from the exuberance of downhill skiing. A simple timber structure coupled with copper-clad columns and red cedar siding give a rustic, yet modern nod to the great outdoors.

FACING PAGE: The dining room offers panoramic views of the slopes of Whistler, Blackcomb, and Wedge Mountains and the emerald water of the glacier-fed lake. The entryway leads directly into this area so guests can immediately embrace the pristine setting.
Photographs by Peter Powles

Since its founding in 1989, John Henshaw Architect Inc. has focused on one idea: that each project should have its own soul. The concept centers on the delicate balance between form and function, which requires an acute sensitivity to every detail and ultimately relates back to the personality, desires, and lifestyle of the homeowner. From the layout of each room to the proper placement of a towel ring, every element must meet both purposeful and aesthetic requirements.

John Henshaw knows the combination poses a unique challenge to each project, but that's what thrills him about architecture. In carrying out the goals and vision for the home, he and his staff pay particular attention to the lighting—both artificial and natural—and the flow or movement throughout a building. Within their wide range of experience, the architects also have a unique understanding of how to appropriately blend Western and Eastern design characteristics; one of the partners and some staff members also speak Mandarin and Cantonese. Whatever the resulting style, a John Henshaw residence is at once comfortable and delightful.

"Architecture has to be experienced, not just viewed."
—John Henshaw

JOHN HENSHAW ARCHITECT

"The urge to build seems to be innate in all of us."

—John Henshaw

RIGHT: Nestled into the crest of a ridge that rises up from Burrard Inlet, the summer home enjoys panoramic views of the water and mountains on the north shore. We used stone to connect the home to the ground and strong horizontal planes of the roof to provide protection from the rain.
Photograph by Janis Nicolay Photography

PREVIOUS PAGES: Suffused with natural light, the spacious living area of a heritage loft penthouse faces south and east to capture the sun and fabulous city views. We planned for roller blinds to allow for summer shading and privacy. White walls and ceiling, glass, stainless steel, and aluminum suggest lightness, while the dark wood and tile give warmth.
Photographs by Michael Boland Photography

"It's all about light."

—John Henshaw

RIGHT: We paid careful attention to natural and artificial lighting, even calling for an automated lighting control system. Within the spa area—where a sauna, hot tub, changing room, and shower complement the pool—concealed cove lighting sets a calming mood. In the home, we also included a climate-controlled wine room, which becomes an elegant showpiece with the wall lighting and spotlights.

FACING PAGE: Since the home is meant for entertaining, we wanted to combine elegance and luxury with comfort—all while exploring a contemporary modern design. A mini resort was the solution. Natural materials—stone, copper, and fir—anchor the authentic palette of materials. Richness, texture, and color are then added through the finishing elements, such as the inlaid wood veneers, marble, granite, stainless steel, artwork, and furniture.

Photographs by Janis Nicolay Photography

"Vision is the ability to look backward and forward and see how we fit into the cultural phenomenon."

—John Henshaw

ABOVE: An older Vancouver home provided a special opportunity for us to re-imagine the rooms for maximum spaciousness, light, and views. We dissected, deconstructed, punctured, pushed, and pulled until everything was perfect. An open-riser staircase with glass railings is just one example of how we opened up the previously constricting spaces.

ABOVE & FACING PAGE: We extended the home visually into the backyard through floor-to-ceiling windows and sliding patio doors that connect to outdoor living spaces. The use of natural materials inside—such as the beautiful marble strata fireplace—enhance the connection to nature, too.
Photographs by Janis Nicolay Photography

"Using natural products from the surrounding locale makes houses seem more inherent to the landscape."

—John Henshaw

TOP & FACING PAGE TOP: Indoor comfort stems from a contemporary use of space combined with the traditional style and craftsmanship of the 1920s-era, Shaughnessy-style home. Exterior elements—painted wood, textured stucco, stone, and cottage windows—mark the uniquely Vancouver style.
Photographs by John Henshaw

MIDDLE, BOTTOM & FACING PAGE BOTTOM: Inspired by a book by A. J. Downing about country homes, the cottage-style residence became a country house in the city. High-quality construction with an airtight envelope ensures the home is energy-efficient, comfortable, and healthy to live in. We integrated Chinese Feng Shui principles into a North American-style home and lifestyle.
Photographs by Janis Nicolay Photography

A house should have a special relationship with its site. More than simply fitting onto the available land, the residence needs to take its cues from the landscape, the views, and the surrounding homes or buildings. Keith Baker, principal of the award-winning KB Design, begins every project based on this philosophy, using a holistic approach to design an appropriate home with natural materials that impart authenticity, both inside and out.

His experience with high-quality millwork—including a full apprenticeship that gave him insight into how the details come together to create the whole—and an innate understanding of design inform his projects. Focusing on quality rather than quantity, Keith and his team employ classic principles in a modern context that will stand the test of time. In collaboration with the homeowners—who are considered participating members of the team—KB Design creates dwellings that tend to positively enrich the lives of the residents living within.

"Details are the subtleties and character reflected throughout the home, making the whole greater than the sum of its parts."

—Keith Baker

KB DESIGN

"Good design is like a good piece of art; it will engage your attention."

—Keith Baker

TOP LEFT & FACING PAGE: Gorgeous views of an ocean inlet prompted us to develop a close relationship with nature through floor-to-ceiling glazing and high, raked clerestory windows. The open-concept kitchen, dining, and living areas—which are all modest in scale to establish warmth—exist as individual rooms yet still allow family and friends to stay visually connected.

LEFT: Overlooking a south-facing Zen garden, the master bath is both private and connected to nature, at once spa-like and contemporary. The glass shower on the right also overlooks the garden; the commode is enclosed with opaque glass.

PREVIOUS PAGES: A long, narrow lot directed us to use an L-shaped floorplan, which we designed around existing trees. Stone, galvanized corrugated steel, and clear western red cedar siding uphold an asymmetrical roof that boasts clean lines and a bit of lightheartedness with an upturned lower edge.
Photographs by Vince Klassen

"The authentic beauty of natural materials grounds a home, making it feel as if it belongs."

—Keith Baker

RIGHT: The undulating site with rocky outcrops and beautiful views of Mount Baker calls for a splayed design and terraced levels, capturing the vistas and allowing the home to gently climb the hillside. Slightly turned away from the street, the simple garage doors virtually disappear amidst the recyclable metal and cedar siding. Organically, the home melts into the land with the help of xeriscape landscaping. With an elevation above the street, passersby are prevented from peering into the living spaces.
Photograph by Vince Klassen

"Designers can be compared to musicians: both work with various rhythm through a creative process. One is with aural elements; the other, physical."

—Keith Baker

RIGHT: The entry atrium's grand but welcoming stairs and five-foot-wide Douglas fir door establish a sense of volume and scale that defines the residence. A durable tile floor and quarter-sawn, American cherry hall closet embrace both function and form. The plethora of windows throughout the terraced levels beckons guests in and up.

FACING PAGE: The contemporary home's open floorplan facilitates a delicate balance between spaciousness for entertaining and intimacy for daily living. With a focus on natural light—as well as features like the open shelving unit that connects the adjoining atrium—the kitchen, dining, and living areas are inviting. Managed-forest jatoba flooring, bamboo cabinetry, low-voltage lighting, and a cast-on-site concrete eating bar create feelings of warmth and responsibility.

Photographs by Vince Klassen

ABOVE: Because of the site's intimate size, we were careful not to overwhelm the streetscape while still giving the homeowners the individuality they desired. Natural materials—stained western red cedar, local stone, and glass—along with the front elevation reduce the home's perceived presence and increase its interest.

LEFT & FACING PAGE BOTTOM: Warm materials, natural light, skylights, glass railings, and steel single stringer stairs maximize the space and lend an open feel throughout the home.

FACING PAGE TOP: Tall sliding Douglas fir doors usher in the outdoors, extending the living areas to the surroundings, which feel secluded with the placement of trees and the use of a partially solid balcony railing. We used a three-sided gas fireplace to continue the connection between the spaces inside.

Photographs by Vince Klassen

Abstract concepts and a lively exchange of ideas are the intellectual sparks that ignite Brad Lamoureux, founder of West Vancouver's renowned Lamoureux Architect Incorporated. Beyond his passion for designing the physical construct of a dwelling, Brad has a love for the personal process of expressing the homeowners' vision by creating environments that resonate with their lives.

Raised in Edmonton, Alberta, Brad received his bachelor's in architecture from Montana State University and earned his master's in architecture at Harvard. Brad also studied social housing and furniture design at the University of Copenhagen where he developed an affinity for organic modernism attributed to Finland's Alvar Aalto, among other architectural styles and genres experienced in his travels. After a few years of designing penthouses, institutional, and commercial work in New York City, Brad moved to West Vancouver in 1987 to focus on residential projects.

His diverse portfolio exemplifies a non-prescriptive style, deep respect for nature and noble aim to design houses that connect with their surroundings. From property selection to groundbreaking approaches, refinement of technical and aesthetic details to coordination and close collaboration, Brad's firm is committed to designing contemporary habitats that define Vancouver's architectural landscape.

"Difficult properties with multiple views and topographic challenges provide amazing creative inspiration."

—Brad Lamoureux

LAMOUREUX ARCHITECT INCORPORATED

"The West Coast vernacular with wide windows and post-and-beam construction really lends itself to sites where the structure must harmoniously coexist with nature."

—Brad Lamoureux

LEFT: We planned the living room and kitchen to be a large singular space simply defined by one column and modern furniture. Indigenous Douglas fir beams, black slate flooring, and African anigre wood combine to create an expression of visual continuity.
Photographs by Derek Lepper

FACING PAGE: Our architectural design underscores the principle that the site informs a building's massing and proportions. A concrete plinth centers the post-and-beam construction and the garage rooftop becomes a foreground garden to be seen as one looks out toward the mountains-meet-ocean vista. We specified slate floors and expansive sliding glass windows for the open-concept home that flows seamlessly from interior spaces to the terrace's oversized hot tub.
Photograph by Derek Lepper

PREVIOUS PAGES: We designed a butterfly roof that opens up to the sky for our "upside-down" house situated on an inaccessible precipice, so the new 5,000-square-foot structure relates beautifully to its natural surroundings. After initial site analysis, we deduced that an iconic wood and steel, West Coast-style house would connect well with densely forested property and offer scenic views of sea and mountains from every vantage point.
Previous pages left photograph by Derek Lepper
Previous pages right photograph by Brad Lamoureux

"Homes that look thoughtfully designed never come together instantaneously; the architecture evolves as the project unfolds."

—Brad Lamoureux

ABOVE: We collaborate well with builders, interior designers, and specialty artisans. Local lumber brokers helped us source centuries-old, tight-grained Douglas fir from our province for the majority of the structure, and we also selected ultra high-grade cherry for complementary flooring and cabinetry. The impressive window frames, floors, and beams were hand-glued and doweled using Japanese joinery techniques. Designs with enduring materials and skillful engineering last for generations. For example, a chimney armature serves as a lateral anchor to withstand an unforeseen earthquake.

RIGHT: Athletic homeowners decided to forgo an elevator, so we designed a tri-level native wood staircase. It ascends to the top of the site so you can view the unspoiled landscape out to the ocean. We incorporate eco-friendly aesthetics, as well as use coated low e-glass, rainwater collection systems, deep overhangs for shade, various passive systems, and sustainable materials.

FACING PAGE: Perched on a rugged granite outcrop amid native cedar and fir trees, the steep site allowed for only one access entry. We elevated the house above the forest line to enjoy views of the ocean beyond. The terraced structure features a concrete plinth that encloses the entry, garage, and gym, while a two-story wood pavilion on top houses primary living functions optimizing the site's light, views, and privacy factor. To further reflect the homeowners' casual West Coast lifestyle, we added a manicured lawn on the garage roof for a grassy play area.
Photographs by Peter Powles

"Transformative renovations with strategically placed elements are as exciting as designing a whole new house."

—Brad Lamoureux

RIGHT: We added expansive windows to the house poised on massive rock for an airy feeling, and to make the bedroom suite feel much larger than it is. Post-and-beam construction helps to support a floor plate that projects out over the slope; it appears to float above the site. The curving stone terrace establishes a connection between house and land, anchored by a meditative lotus pond that collects rainwater, spilling a waterfall into the reflecting pool at the base of the master suite.

FACING PAGE: A contemporary 1950s post-and-beam home was strong in its own right, but we took it to new heights, adding on a Japanese-inspired pavilion with master bedroom suite, central closet and bath, expanded art gallery space, and stone terrace. Already a recognized structure in the region, we enhanced the architecture to meld with natural colors from its granite bluff site. The house possesses distinctive character while still being connected to its origins, accomplished by marrying old and new building forms. A cantilevered glass canopy and triangular skylight lets dwellers see the towering trees outside. The home now makes a statement as a light-filled gallery to showcase the homeowner's prized art collection.

Photographs by Ed White

"Simplicity is innovation."

—Brad Lamoureux

LEFT: A fine artist and modern art collector wanted to display his valuable sculpture positioned above the bedroom fireplace. We drew plans for a direct-vent gas fireplace housed in clear maple cabinetry as opposed to a wood-burning unit with a tall chimney shaft. As a result, smoke and soot are a non-issue and the piece can be admired by the resident art connoisseur.

FACING PAGE: Based on the homeowner's desire to maximize the scenic views and create as much space as possible for displaying art, we devised plans for a freestanding, sculptural building-within-a-building as part of the master suite addition. The clear maple structure includes a walk-in closet that separates the bedroom from the bathroom. A custom bed and night tables are built into one wall to economize on clutter. By using restraint and simply having basic elements, the art dominates. The original mid-century post-and-beam structure was retained and replicated in the master bedroom addition. The original grey stacked fieldstone chimney breast also remains and provides textural contrast in the main living space.
Photographs by Ed White

Architect Tony Kloepfer certainly appreciates modern technological advances; however, he understands and respects age-old philosophies and techniques that have proven successful time and time again. In leading Scientific Architecture, Tony ensures every project embraces one underlying principle that dates back to Marcus Vitruvius Pollio, a first-century BC Roman writer, architect, and engineer: architecture must accommodate and delight.

From this idea springs forth the importance that the home should be specifically fitted to the residents and their unique lifestyle, leaning to their tastes while incorporating good design principles and refreshing, timeless elements. From there, Scientific Architecture purposefully combines art and science, aesthetics and function.

Of equal importance is the responsibility to use resources efficiently, carefully considering the entire ecological footprint of a house's design-build-habitation life cycle. Materials are chosen based on ecological impact, elements are reused when possible, and proper design is implemented to reduce energy and resource consumption, with the whole building planned for longevity. In essence, every wall, every beam, every space must enhance how the homeowners will live in the home, both today and far into the future.

"The framing of a view should be as important as the view itself."

—Tony Kloepfer

SCIENTIFIC ARCHITECTURE

ABOVE: Mosaic tiles suggesting a tidal pool are set within the basalt tile flooring to provide an infusion of bright color at the base of the custom glass artwork that greets everyone upon entering the Sea Lion Pointe villa. We used the fireplace to separate the sunken living room on the main level from the games mezzanine above.
Photograph by Jad Davenport

FACING PAGE: We organized the Sea Lion Pointe villa into two main wings: public living areas and private sleeping spaces. The living areas are anchored by the massive fireplace that features a commissioned triptych painting, naturally lit from above. Custom wrought iron railings in a dragonfly motif and a suspended art glass mobile invoking the nearby underwater kelp forests incorporate the outdoors.
Photograph by Darren Bernhaerdt

PREVIOUS PAGES: For the renovation project of Eagle Rock Lodge on Sonora Island, rich wood elements took center stage as we replaced the existing metal-framed windows. Installing extensive wood casing and structural supports bring visual warmth to the living room, outlining the spectacular views. In the large master bedroom, natural materials provide an enhanced level of intimacy that harmonizes with the surrounding lush forest.
Photographs by Darren Bernhaerdt

"The entrance should act as an introduction to a building, like an overture to a symphony."

—Tony Kloepfer

ABOVE, TOP RIGHT & FACING PAGE: Overlooking the ocean and immersed in nature on Sonora Island, the 11,000-square-foot villa was carefully sited to achieve optimal views. We utilized a staged construction process with a crane to protect the landscape and retain as much of the natural forest as possible. The design intent was to diminish the boundary between the interior and exterior spaces through expansive glass walls under soaring, timber-framed roofs. Throughout, the villa is linked to nature by a series of finished indoor and unfinished outdoor story poles, conveying the notion of a polished interior leading to a rugged exterior.

ABOVE: Featuring open glazing on three sides to capture ocean views and sunlight, the living room windows are composed into a structural rhythm with larger support posts and beams; a subtle secondary mullion pattern lines up with the doorways. We sited a gazebo nearby, echoing a similar but more exposed structure incorporating Japanese wood framing. *Photographs by Darren Bernhaerdt*

"A simple palette of rich, natural materials can provide a harmonious unity that ties together the various functions and spaces of a home."

—Tony Kloepfer

ABOVE: We softened the coldness of industrial stainless steel appliances with warm Douglas fir wood cabinetry and basalt tile flooring. A fully glazed side wall provides natural light and ocean views beyond the covered outdoor dining area, further blurring the line between interior and exterior living spaces.
Photograph by Darren Bernhaerdt

RIGHT: Cast glass light fixtures hang like bubbles over the bathtub. The isolated setting of the villa offered us the opportunity to design each space specifically to take advantage of the views and provide total privacy while allowing fully glazed walls in each of the four ensuite bathrooms.
Photograph by Darren Bernhaerdt

FACING PAGE TOP: Blurring the boundary between interior and exterior spaces can be accomplished not only through extensive glazing but also by extending the roof structure and locating elements—such as the carved story poles—both inside and outside the window plane.
Photograph by Jad Davenport

FACING PAGE BOTTOM: Part of the design process is determining how best to showcase the homeowner's art collection, including incorporating display niches lined with complementary materials and feature lighting.
Photograph by Darren Bernhaerdt

"The simplest solutions
are often the most
ecologically beneficial."

—Tony Kloepfer

TOP LEFT: We strive to insert buildings and landscaping carefully to enhance the site rather than create a distraction from the spectacular natural setting.
Photograph by Jad Davenport

LEFT: Even though the adjacent buildings are constructed of different material than the conservatory greenhouse—wood timber versus a glazed aluminum structure—similarities bring cohesion. We incorporated consistent roof slopes, exposed truss design, and stone piers throughout all of the buildings.
Photograph by Darren Bernhaerdt

FACING PAGE: A careful evaluation of a building site includes determining optimal views. In one living room at Gillard Lodge of Sonora Resort, we provided extra height to allow the full expanse of the natural setting to come to life. In another instance, an adjacent building to the left prompted us to raise the living room while lowering the deck in front to keep the ocean view unobstructed.
Photographs by Darren Bernhaerdt

Combining luxury with function is no easy task. It takes an innate sense of design and a certain dedication to ensure both ideas are carefully woven into a unified aesthetic. For Andy Friesen, founder and principal of Su Casa Design, blending the two seemingly contradictory concepts has always been a priority. He appreciates the desire for beauty, yet knows that incorporating the homeowner's lifestyle is as important as the design style.

Within every beautifully designed home, the team at Su Casa Design uses flow and natural light to enhance the functionality of any space, welcoming homeowners and their guests to comfortably enjoy every area. Andy and his staff establish a rhythm between rooms and devise innovative solutions to ensure a cohesive layout. At the same time, an abundance of windows take advantage of whatever view is available, flooding the home with sunlight and connecting the indoors with the outdoors. Each design is not only visually stunning but also includes spaces that will be useful for decades to come.

"Regardless of size, a home needs to exude a certain degree of practicality."

—Andy Friesen

SU CASA DESIGN

"Natural light is key to the lifeline of a home."

—Andy Friesen

TOP RIGHT: Instead of the typical two-story foyer with a traditional stairwell and balcony, I created a viewpoint from the library down into the foyer below. Vaulted ceilings in the library were added for even more drama. The oval opening adds interest and connects the levels of the home in an unconventional manner.

RIGHT & FACING PAGE: Amazing views are captured through huge windows; light, fresh colors allow the great room to appear formal but not stuffy. To lend an open feel without creating the bowling alley effect, I designed the dining room as a buffer between the kitchen and great room, using a two-way fireplace on one end and a see-through china buffet on the other. The kitchen continues the airy feel but with a little more warmth. The stove hood, a stunning feature, is made of wood finished with metallic paint.

PREVIOUS PAGES: The layout was driven by two goals: capture breathtaking views of nearby Mount Baker from the rear and allow the front driveway to be seen from inside, particularly from the kitchen—which I placed in the center under the eyebrow roof. In order to achieve an elegant, yet not pretentious, residence that fit into its surroundings, I designed the exterior to resemble a French Country cottage.

Photographs by Jason Brown

"The first step in home design is to determine what the property has to offer."

—Andy Friesen

LEFT: Although the home was sited among traditional dwellings, the homeowner preferred a contemporary, clean aesthetic. I took cues from classic forms but pared down the finishes for a fresh, simple look.

FACING PAGE TOP: A wide estate property called for a sprawling floorplan, with a main focus on accommodating large gatherings. The long driveway leads guests up to the grand front entrance but also through a portico into an auto court and four-car garage.

FACING PAGE BOTTOM: The elegant estate home's classic brick aesthetic suggests timelessness. I planned the home to be long and narrow so that every room overlooks the infinity pool, private lake, and breathtaking snow-covered mountains.

Photographs by Jason Brown

"The main entry should entice people in and give them a hint of what the rest of the home is all about."

—Andy Friesen

RIGHT: My vision was to create a Tudor-like cottage without all of the busy exterior woodwork of a typical Tudor home. Through textured stucco, stonework, and black-framed windows, I maintained the desired character but simplified the elements. I also used a bell-cast roof reminiscent in French and English design. The tall central window allows the staircase to be filled with natural light; inside, a curved barrel ceiling follows the window's shape.
Photograph by Jason Brown

"Staying within the box is comfortable; I prefer to expand the box and show people what's possible."

—Andy Friesen

RIGHT: After examining the property's five fully forested mountainside acres, I placed the home on the highest point to ensure views of the meandering creek that encompasses three sides of the home. Every room was designed to take advantage of the outdoors, standing true to the homeowner's wish of seeing nature from every angle. Even in the powder room, the layout works with the window placement. The lime green quartz countertop makes reference to the green tiles in the kitchen and adds a punch of funk to the simple, small space.

FACING PAGE TOP: The West Coast contemporary feel of the home is seen immediately in the main entry, where a concrete feature wall and glass railings surround the suspended stairwell to the lower level. I utilized a large window wall to overlook a sunken fern and rock-bed garden.

FACING PAGE BOTTOM: In the modern, fresh kitchen, multiple sets of doors can open up to the outside; in winter, the glass allows for that constant connection. A hint of lime green in the glass tile backsplash brings in enough color to animate the space.
Photographs by Jason Brown

WoodRose Homes' principal Jim Vance views himself as an extension of the homeowner, the architect, and the interior designer. Yet he doesn't just follow the blueprint for a project. Instead, he seeks to understand the vision of the project and philosophy of the architect or designer—to see what is intended beyond the two-dimensional lines of the plans. Along with his extensive experience, a deeper understanding of the project affords him the knowledge to catch potential issues before they arise and ensure the physical manifestation of the design matches the original vision.

Of particular note in a home by WoodRose is the level of quality that is found not only in the finishes that are seen every day but also in the materials that are essential to the home but aren't seen, like the studs, drywall, and insulation. Achieved through a creative, resourceful team of project managers and superintendents who are dedicated to craftsmanship, the team's high standards result in quieter, warmer, and more comfortable homes that spark a sense of awe in even the most discerning homeowner.

"The behind-the-scenes substance is as important as the surface finishes; otherwise it'd be like hanging the Mona Lisa on a tent wall."

—Jim Vance

WOODROSE HOMES

"Vision is a much deeper concept than only understanding what you're able to see physically."

—Jim Vance

LEFT, FACING PAGE, & PREVIOUS PAGES: The home's location on a hillside overlooking picturesque Vancouver and Mount Baker provided a wonderful sun-filled western exposure. Blending contemporary aesthetics with traditional details, Leslie Balagno with HB Design Consultants specified that we use a vast amount of rich cherry paneling with contemporary grooves. Surprisingly, even though traditional homes typically involve more ornate work, projects that focus on modern design techniques provide a unique challenge because inconsistencies stand out among the smooth textures and long lines.

Photographs by Philip Jarmain Photography

"The best homes are built by blending an understanding of the architect's intent with the homeowner's anticipated use of its spaces."

—Jim Vance

RIGHT: Throughout the hillside home, we used natural materials—limestone, marble, cherry wood—both inside and out to enhance the connection to nature. Green building techniques, including a geothermal energy system, were employed when possible.
Photograph by Philip Jarmain Photography

"Quality is a measurable element, but it has little to do with a dollar sign."

—Jim Vance

RIGHT & FACING PAGE: Initially designed by Lamoureux Architect Incorporated in 2000, the plans for a waterfront home in West Vancouver had to be put on hold. Years later, the homeowners were able to revisit the idea of building the house; they wanted to keep the original architecture and interior design by Brad Lamoureux, but at a substantial cost reduction. Working with both the architect and the homeowners, we were able to significantly reduce the price by revisiting which details were nonessential to the French Provincial design, while keeping the important ones like the handmade zinc roof shingles and the beautiful circular staircase.
Photographs by Brad Lamoureux

"A project should result in a home, not a crystal palace that's difficult to feel comfortable in."

—Jim Vance

RIGHT: Our goal is to carry out the architect and interior designer's plans, but it's important for us to understand the future residents. Knowing how they will interact within the home helps us deliver the right details and finishes to facilitate the way they will use the spaces.
Photograph by Brad Lamoureux

Whistler Interior Design, page 105

Jake James, page 125

elements of structure

Principal Debbie Evans and her team at Whistler Interior Design give undivided attention to each project, so it's not surprising that the firm was selected to help design the 2010 Winter Olympics Athlete's Village in Whistler. With more than two decades in architecture, construction, and decorating, Debbie knows how to create solutions that far exceed expectations—both functionally and aesthetically—while also staying within budget. Of particular importance to clientele who may not live nearby, the firm's detailed processes and technical systems ensure homeowners are kept abreast of the work even if they cannot physically visit the site. And Debbie's relationship with talented artisans means even the most bespoke designs can be accommodated.

Whether working with a bachelor or a large family, or on projects ranging from the blueprint stage on a new construction to an update of an existing home, Debbie and her team's passion for interior and millwork design and project management is evident. They have even been known to prepare a home for the family's arrival from overseas by decorating it for the upcoming Christmas season, lighting the fireplace, and stocking the refrigerator—truly the epitome of service.

"Following the lines of the house and improving upon them is crucial to good design."

—Debbie Evans

WHISTLER INTERIOR DESIGN

"Architecture speaks to me and reveals the most harmonious path of design."

—Debbie Evans

ABOVE & FACING PAGE: We transformed a dreary kitchen into a bright, updated space that accommodates multiple families in the matriarch's home. Removing a wall that was located next to the refrigerator created more room to move within the area and allows family members to play games at the table while numerous cooks prepare food around the large island. Natural, earthy materials, like the soapstone countertops, establish a beautiful connection to nature. We added lots of storage—including bookshelves by the refrigerator, drawers in the side of the island, and cabinets flanking the banquette—to house games, books, and other items to keep guests entertained. An oversized bar area provides another space for guests to be socially involved but out of the cooks' way.

PREVIOUS PAGES: Sited on 42 acres, the log home focuses on capturing the views and establishing a warm, rustic ambience. We worked closely with the architect from the initial planning stages to ensure every detail was in line with the overall aesthetic. Large windows, terra cotta colors, a tree root island, exposed tree bark accents, and stone cut into the wood flooring bring the outdoors in. The large stone arch ties the kitchen to other areas in the home where stone plays a central role in the design.

Photographs by Insight Photography

"Design success is
determined by how well
the project reflects the
homeowner's desires."

—Debbie Evans

LEFT: Our renovation of an existing home was based upon the homeowner's
collection of bronze Buddhist statues that did not fit well in the original
rustic style. We streamlined the spaces and brightened them up through
white trim and a plethora of custom lighting. Every detail was added to
specifically accommodate the homeowner's needs, such as the lighting in
the art niche.
Photograph by Insight Photography

"Regardless of the style, a home can be designed to look fresh and appealing decades from now."

—Debbie Evans

ABOVE, RIGHT & FACING PAGE: After working on four previous projects with the homeowner, we were familiar with his style and taste. Instead of following what he had done in previous projects, we encouraged him to try something different—and he was ecstatic about the final result. We blended West Coast style with a bit of Asian flair to give a clean but warm appearance, which was unorthodox when we designed the home more than a decade ago. Lots of glass and stone was used throughout the spaces to give a sense of continuity. The home overlooks ski runs on Whistler Mountain, so privacy was of utmost importance. We utilized various retaining walls, solid railings, and other privacy screens to allow the homeowner to see out but keep others from peering inside.

Photographs by Insight Photography

"The intimacy of the bathroom becomes an icon of personal luxury, an individual creative expression."

—Julia Ilnitchi

ABOVE: Because we believe the bathroom is a space worthy of the utmost attention, every collection brings back the pleasurable feel of materials. The Seventy collection, an Italian design, is no exception. Rounded edges, smooth surfaces, and integrated handles evoke a cozy, tranquil feel that blends with the soft colors. The seamless vanity with integrated sinks provides both function and beauty.

FACING PAGE: Always mindful of ecological concerns, we offer mirrors that are not only aesthetically pleasing but respectful of the environment. The mirror is free from copper and formaldehyde, and has a low lead and solvent content. The epoxy powder varnish protects the surface from scratches and is 10 times more resistant to corrosion than normal finishes. *Photographs courtesy of Ambient Bathrooms*

"Exceptional materials, design, and finishes blend beautifully to create a room devoted to relaxation and wellbeing."

—Julia Ilnitchi

ABOVE: Designed as an evolution of the bathroom, the City collection evokes excitement and surprise through a refined atmosphere. I love working with this Italian collection because of its versatility to adapt to any space and style. With a variety of designer colors and finishes, every taste can be accommodated. In a sleek space, glossy lacquer cabinetry is paired with an extra-clear glass countertop, integrated washbasin, and tall units, all in a monochromatic hue.

FACING PAGE TOP: Our extra-clear glass countertop is made from leaded glass that is completely transparent; even when color is added, the hue is pure with no color alterations. By pouring melted glass into a mold, firing it in a kiln, and then sandblasting and varnishing it if necessary, the curved glass basin is created with excellent quality. The integrated countertops can also be created with two sinks in both regular and curved cabinetry. My favorite feature, though, is the functional drawer directly beneath the sink; a cutout for the plumbing underneath allows this typically unused space to become functional again.

FACING PAGE BOTTOM: Tall units in a glossy lacquer and bronze glass provide abundant, out-of-the-way storage that is lit from inside.
Photographs courtesy of Ambient Bathrooms

"The bathroom is often the space where you start and end your day, so it should be characterized by aesthetic equilibrium and fluid harmonies."

—Julia Ilnitchi

ABOVE, RIGHT & FACING PAGE: One of my favorite aspects of the TreEasy collection is the use of vertical wood grain on narrow drawers, creating a beautiful, modern effect. Available in various combinations that can dramatically change the overall aesthetic, the furniture unites pure lines with innovative materials. A popular ecological option is a countertop made of Idropan, a 100-percent recycled wood panel that resists moisture expansion. To enhance the contemporary feel, the top and the cabinetry were lacquered in an ultra-matte finish. By combining vertical and horizontal lines in one space, we created an elegant ambience, whereas the composition featuring a stainless steel accent on the grey-toned countertop leg embraces modernity.

Photographs courtesy of Ambient Bathrooms

DECORATIVE PAINTING & PLASTERING CONCEPTS

"Plaster can turn an ordinary wall into a masterpiece, bringing life to an otherwise static space."

—Darrell Morrison

ABOVE: For centuries, natural lime plaster has been the choice for a finish material in the world's finest homes. It has many outstanding traits, including its antifungal properties and a green makeup that includes little or no VOCs, not to mention its versatility and durability. The material even has the ability to wrap around corners and curves, and we can recreate any color or texture, from stone to fabric. In situations where heavy materials like stone are impractical or impossible to use, like with the master bathroom's groin vault ceiling, lime plaster can provide a near-perfect replica. Even the exact color and veining of a high-end natural stone can be reproduced. We use only the highest-quality, imported Italian lime plaster in our installations and always apply it by hand so that we can flawlessly control the color, texture, and sheen.

FACING PAGE: With a majority of ceilings over 11 feet high, the home boasts an amazing amount of detail with a decidedly Tuscan villa feel. Taking cues from the Old World furniture, we used an intonachino finish for a rustic, pitted texture and matte sheen.
Photographs by Jason Brown

"What makes beautiful plaster come to life isn't just the sheen or the color; it's the ability to incorporate a vision into a piece of art that will last a lifetime and beyond."

—Darrell Morrison

ABOVE: In keeping with the home's Tuscan villa atmosphere, the homeowners wanted a specific Old World pattern on the wine room's ceiling. Unable to find the exact motif that they wanted in tin or copper, they brought us in to create the specific look through plaster. We applied vinyl decals over the entire 350-square-foot ceiling, carefully laying each square-foot piece down one at a time for precise placement. Then we laid the plaster over the decals, going back and forth on each piece to pull out the appropriate finish. The entire process took almost a month to complete, but the end result—a beautiful masterpiece—was well worth the work.

FACING PAGE: We installed more than 4,000 square feet of plaster in the residence, which added a sanitary element to the home because of plaster's antimicrobial properties. The warm beige color and deep rustic texture on the dining room walls and ceiling speak directly to the Tuscan villa ambience.
Photographs by Jason Brown

"A home is more than just a place to reside; when finished with the right materials, it can visually transport you to faraway places."

—Darrell Morrison

ABOVE & TOP RIGHT: To create the look of an 18th-century New York City bank vault, the builder installed carved wooden blocks. We then covered them with a matte plaster and finished with a glaze for an aged appearance. The large sconces flanking the doorway feature the smooth-to-the-touch carrara marmorino finish.

BOTTOM RIGHT: Plaster allows us the ability to cover directly over drywall or wood for an amazing impact without a massive restructure or enforcement of the wall. The intonachino treatment on the wall gives the appearance of cinder blocks without the weight.

FACING PAGE TOP & BOTTOM LEFT: When properly applied, lime plaster is an ideal product for a fireplace because it can withstand the heat. Its durability is unmatched, too. Depending on the project, we use upwards of four layers of plaster. The true beauty of lime plaster is its continual hardening, making it stronger as it ages.

FACING PAGE BOTTOM RIGHT: Because it's naturally resistant to mildew and fungus, lime plaster is appropriate for use in moist environments, like bathrooms. To enhance the aesthetic value, we can even apply unique textures and colors, as we did in the home on the Pacific Ocean where the finish resembles ripples of water. Adding waxes and metallic pigments can also create a stunning, one-of-a-kind finish.
Photographs by Jason Brown

"Forging involves a dynamic power that captures the process within the finished artwork."

—Jake James

ABOVE & FACING PAGE: In contrast to cast metal, which is molten and then poured into a mold, or machined metal, which is cut away from a larger piece, forged metal is heated to a plastic point and then manipulated with force. The result is massive structural strength, perfect for a stair railing. To create the geometric, masculine design with a lotus that the homeowner wanted, I used thick spindles and deep reliefs within the flower. Traditional blacksmith joinery techniques—rivets and mortise and tenons—add visual depth to the three-story, 60-foot-long railing.
Photographs by Merle Proflofsky

"Blacksmithing is deeply fulfilling because it deals with fire and pressure, elemental forces that shaped the world."

—Jake James

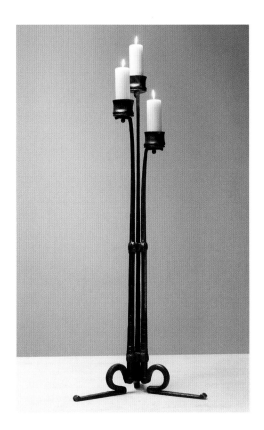

ABOVE LEFT: An asymmetrical candle stand nearly five feet tall combines physical mass with elegance.
Photograph by Doug Gilbert

ABOVE MIDDLE: Fluidity isn't typically associated with metal, but blacksmithing allows me to gently curve steel into very organic designs. For the freeform nature of the staircase panel, I worked with each piece individually, letting the design evolve along the way.
Photograph by Doug Gilbert

ABOVE RIGHT: To give the illusion of a deciduous tree in a windstorm, I forged a certain degree of movement into the five-foot-tall coat rack with forms representing the wind and leaves swirling around the tree.
Photograph by Doug Gilbert

FACING PAGE: Standing more than seven feet tall, the 600-pound gate was designed and built in collaboration with two other blacksmiths—Jeff Holtby and Jorgen Harle—for a gallery exhibition. We used European-style forging and heavy texture as the basis for the design. The frameless nature rejects the traditional idea of a gate, and the fan-like elements illustrate how the metal reacts to pressure. We passed the vertical bars through the horizontal pieces using a technique called slitting and drifting. To create the aged look and protect it from the elements, a waxed rust finish was applied.
Photograph by Bill Ruth

"Even if executed with subtle details, steel naturally becomes a dominant feature in the space."

—Jake James

ABOVE: Blacksmithing has a rich and lengthy history, yet the process is still applicable, even in modern settings. I forged the ultra-contemporary railing out of steel, using large, cold rolled steel rivets for a precise fit. All of the pieces are finished with a hard wax, which prevents corrosion and wear and gives a smooth, comfortable feel.
Photographs by Jeffery Bosdet

FACING PAGE: Loosely influenced by Asian principles, the forged gate offers a variety of focal points. At four feet wide, it was too large for a single leaf so I utilized asymmetrical sizes for the two doors. The bamboo growing inside the garden provided inspiration, and the forged bamboo on the gate was designed to look as if it were swaying in the wind. The infill bars are heavily textured and scalloped steel. Perfect for an outdoor setting, the gate is finished with rust and then waxed and oiled to prevent the rust from transferring to those who touch the gate.
Photograph by Federico Vanoli

"The kitchen is a gathering place for families and also where people congregate to eat when entertaining—a showpiece that's also used for food preparation."

—Chris Eden

ABOVE: We worked with the tastes of the homeowners, who had a very specific idea in mind—timeless and traditional as opposed to the Tuscan/Southwest look popular in the home's Paradise Valley neighborhood in Phoenix. White cabinetry and soft tones of adjacent materials create comfortable warmth. The cabinetry layout accomplishes flexibility through many work zones and storage areas. The various elements meld to create the perfect space that accommodates entertaining, homework, and enjoying the scenery while cooking at the range.

FACING PAGE: High ceilings in the Tuscan-inspired home dictated our use of large-scale furniture and decorative elements. A beautiful furniture crown with a hand-carved appliqué draws the eye up, while large, hand-carved corbels on the island provide weight so the island doesn't become overpowered by the room. Symmetry and balance are achieved with wrought iron accents and glass door inserts, helping create an inviting space for family and friends to enjoy gourmet food and fine wine.

Photographs by Pam Singleton, Image Photography, LLC

"Kitchens are exquisite because of the variety of rich materials, appliances, backsplashes, lighting, and countertops. Everyone has certain needs and requirements, so no two are ever the same."

—Chris Eden

ABOVE: Designed for entertaining, the large but low-to-the-ground island with carrara marble top and sides encourages guests to visit with the homeowner while food is being prepared. We routed all cabinetry doors to appear as four-drawer cabinets, a technique which carries the eye throughout the kitchen to create a continuous horizontal line accentuating the clean contemporary lines of the marble and appliances. At the bar, we cut out the inside of the shelves and inserted glass for unimpeded downlighting.
Photograph by Pam Singleton, Image Photography, LLC

FACING PAGE TOP: The very linear kitchen fits with the house's contemporary atmosphere and multitude of windows throughout. Glass shelves and the slate countertop contrast the rich earthen espresso maple cabinets. Designed for the cook who entertains, the kitchen's mixture of warm wood and steel gives the guest a feeling of being in a sleek new high-class penthouse.
Photograph by Mike Heywood, Trilogy Studios

FACING PAGE BOTTOM: Designing a functional yet aesthetically pleasing open-concept kitchen provided a few challenges, but we accommodated the family's needs without sacrificing beauty. Island seating, an efficient use of storage space, plenty of usable countertop space, and a dropped cooking area with a custom canopy enhance the entertainment capabilities.
Photograph by Mike Heywood, Trilogy Studios

"Subtle details speak volumes when added in the right place or paired with the perfect complementary element."

—Chris Eden

ABOVE: In a mid-century modern bungalow, the contemporary kitchen was all about clean lines and a unique combination of cool and warm finishes. We brought the high-gloss cabinet hue up to the ceiling to enlarge the feel of the kitchen, and added in a few grey tones to coordinate with the stainless steel appliances and granite countertops. The space featured a nook, seating area, and washer and dryer to accommodate a variety of needs for the family.
Photograph by Luke Moilliet

FACING PAGE: Rearranging some of the appliances, repurposing an unused desk space, and redesigning the island transformed the outdated kitchen into a timeless masterpiece that allows the family of six to comfortably gather. We paired a variety of finishes—including a custom rub on the accented island—to imbue a traditional/transitional blend. The cabinets are a combination of custom and semi-custom work to help with the budget but still maintain a one-of-a-kind look. The kitchen includes all of the family's wish-list appliances for complete modernization: multiple convection ovens, an ice cream maker, a second sink, a new dishwasher, and a Miele coffee maker with pullout countertop for use when flavoring drinks.
Photograph by Pam Singleton, Image Photography, LLC

SOUTH FRASER STAIRS

Surrey, British Columbia

"A staircase is like a nice sculpture within the home, and it brings a certain aesthetic effect through a functional form."

—John Gosek

ABOVE & FACING PAGE: One of my first jobs in Canada was in a stair factory, and although I had worked as a designer in Poland and Germany, I was virtually clueless about the construction process. As I learned how to construct stairs, I was hooked. Some of my favorite projects involve contemporary design, which requires such perfection in its smooth, minimal forms. My fascination stems from the fact that even within two contemporary projects that both utilize similar foundations—open risers and vertical grain white oak for the treads and railings, for example—the details can change the entire look. In a renovated townhouse, housed stringers along the sides of the steps reflect a smooth, substantial look; glass replaces traditional balusters and is inset into the stringers while an unbroken railing runs from the basement to the top floor, offering safety and continuity. A similar second project eliminates the housed stringers, allowing the zig-zag effect of the steps to be seen from the side. Basement-to-top-floor railings also provide continuity in this residence, but the glass is attached directly to the stair treads with stainless steel standoffs.
Photographs by Ivan Hunter

"Because the stairs often are a focal point, they need to coordinate with the style of the home and become more than just a way to get from the lower floor to the upper floors."

—John Gosek

ABOVE: Exotic tiger wood, which conveniently matched the flooring, gave us the durability and stunning beauty we were looking for. A request to install lights into every tread was a challenge, but the result at night is an incredible glowing sculpture accented by a stainless steel railing.

FACING PAGE TOP LEFT & BOTTOM: In the contemporary townhouse, we created railings with declining corners to impart smooth transitions at every turn, aiding in the connected feeling from bottom to top floors. The natural finish shows the beauty of white oak.

FACING PAGE TOP RIGHT: Tempered clear glass instead of balusters allows the gorgeous ocean views to be more easily seen from various parts of the house, but the material requires precise measuring and careful installation on our part. If it's even slightly off, we have no choice but to re-order.

Photographs by Ivan Hunter

LEFT & FACING PAGE: For a traditional house, we designed an extra-wide, closed-riser staircase to resemble the Old World homes of France or Italy. Close collaboration with the interior designer led us to design and craft intricate continuous metal frames and hand railings. We also added mouldings along the stringers and at each landing. Perfectly executed details are central to the design since a large window in the grand foyer floods the area with light.
Photographs by Ivan Hunter

V6B DESIGN GROUP

"Kitchen design should consider and unify the entire home."

—Earl Lawson

ABOVE & FACING PAGE: To extend the comfortable old European feel of the home's main floor to the kitchen, we designed a rustic country French château look. We installed traditional inset-style cabinetry in knotty alder—with very heavy wearing, antiquing, and distressing—and Stratford-style cabinet doors to provide the relaxed, authentic look. The extensive use of mouldings, posts, and glass to provide the finishing touches continues through the back half of the house. The sink wall was planned without wall cabinets to ensure the windows remained featured.
Photographs by David Oliver

"The personality of a space, when properly matched to the home and the residents, will still feel comfortable a decade later."

—Earl Lawson

ABOVE: In a 1920s English Heritage home in Shaughnessy, Vancouver, functional elegance defines the parameters for the kitchen. Anchoring the entire plan, the island maintains open display shelving and a large surface for cooking and family interaction. The lowered hood fan and cabinets accommodate the stained-glass transom windows, highlighting the oven wall as a main feature and design element. The closed grain hardwood in blackstone stain cabinetry bases is softened by the uppers, which are antique white with caramel accents.
Photograph courtesy of V6B Design Group

FACING PAGE TOP: The 12-foot-long oversized island features a stainless steel top for preparation and cleanup. The dark stained, horizontal grained, riftsawn white oak cabinetry remains low in the space so that it doesn't distract from the room's clean contemporary elegance. A quartzite backsplash and antique brushed majestic black granite floors provide grace while maintaining a simplicity that doesn't distract from the penthouse's prominent design elements—the residents' displayed artwork and the spectacular 35th-floor view of the ocean and mountains.
Photographs by David Oliver

FACING PAGE BOTTOM: We chose the finishes to reinforce the comfortable and welcoming look of Provence-style kitchens. The warm tones of the custom plaster hood and walls are the perfect backdrop for the strong French colors in the cabinetry. The soft curves of the dining bar invite guests to gather and visit with the cook.
Photographs by Brian Gill

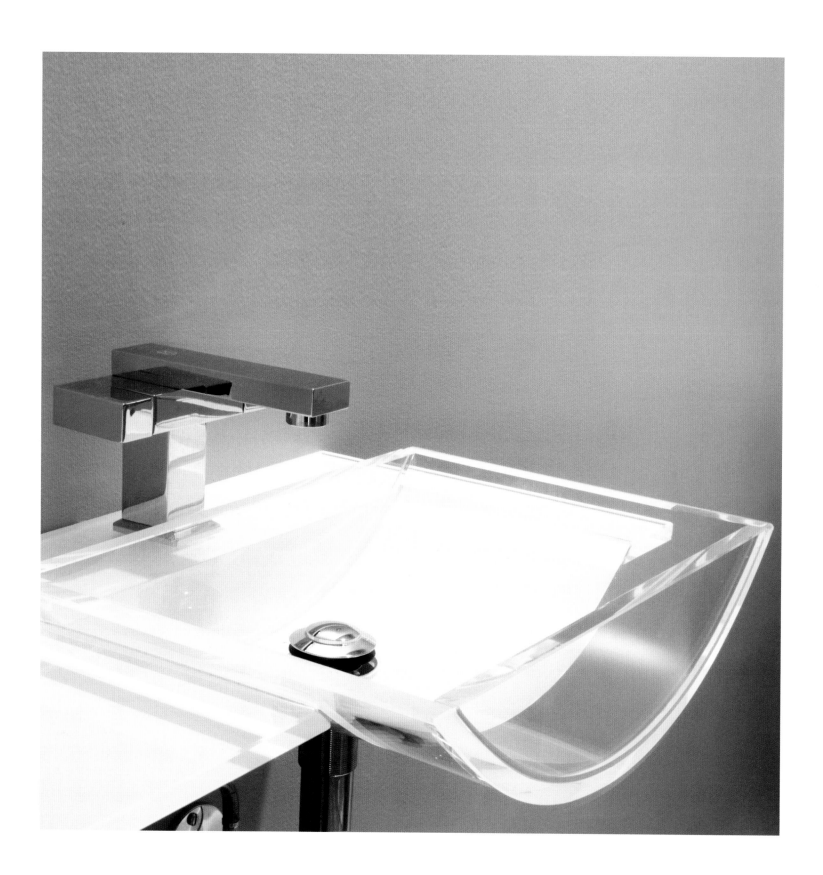

"Glass is an extremely versatile and malleable material. Its structural properties and transparency have become essential to the open concepts of contemporary architectural design."

—Dennis Hrubizna

ABOVE LEFT: Most projects begin with an architect, designer, or homeowner articulating a project's concepts; then, relying on our firm's nearly three decades of experience, we craft a solution that meets the design criteria.

ABOVE RIGHT: Many of our staff members are trained fine artists, so projects that require extensive creativity are approached with excitement. A sleek travertine fireplace is punctuated with a band of glass wrapped around three sides. We stacked multiple thicknesses of glass, similar to building a stone fence, to create an ever-changing design element.

FACING PAGE: In a small powder room, the designer required a fixture that was light and small but would still be functional. We created a countertop and sink that met the challenge and coordinated with the modernist style of the home.
Photographs by Lucas Hrubizna

Douglas Reynolds Gallery, page 151

Michael Trayler Designs, page 157

elements of design

Sublime Interiors, page 163

Tom Bakker Design, page 169

Westcoast Audio Video Gallery, page 175

DOUGLAS REYNOLDS GALLERY

Vancouver, British Columbia

"It's important in any art form that the flow, the balance, and the design interact with each other."

—Douglas Reynolds

ABOVE: Cedar bentwood boxes have been made along the Northwest Coast for many generations. Used for storage, transport, and burial, these works were often decorated with painted and carved designs, as is the contemporary *Bear Bentwood Chest* by Don Yeomans of the Haida Nation.

FACING PAGE: One of the most prominent Haida artists working today, Don Yeomans has become well known for his dramatic use of color and his beautifully fluid formline design. *Killer Whale Panel* is an excellent example of Yeomans' design aesthetic.
Photographs by John Calhoun

"With Native American art from the Northwest Coast, it's important to have historical context, showing how the art has evolved. It is a living art form, and it is very much alive, as is the culture."

—Douglas Reynolds

ABOVE: Kwakwaka'wakw artist Beau Dick is one of the most notable woodcarvers on the Northwest Coast and is regarded as one of the best mask makers. Beautifully rendered with fine tool work, brilliant colors and the addition of cedar bark and feathers, *Grouse Mask* perfectly exhibits his talent.

LEFT: The historic *Gitksan Pole Segment* is the most important historical piece to come into our gallery. The pole has exceptional provenance, and comes from Gitksan territory in northwestern British Columbia. Noted ethnographer Marius Barbeau discussed and photographed this pole in his 1929 book, *Totem Poles of the Gitksan*, and Canadian painter Emily Carr painted the pole in 1928 when she visited the area. Carr's painting is now located in the Glenbow Museum in Calgary.

FACING PAGE: Crooked beak masks are associated with the Kwakwaka'wakw Hamatsa dance ceremony and represent cannibalistic supernatural birds. Stan Hunt III's *Crooked Beak Mask* is made of red cedar.
Photographs by John Calhoun

"It's imperative for people to personally connect with pieces before adding them to their private collections."

—Douglas Reynolds

ABOVE: The 1,700-square-foot gallery is broken into sections via stairs and alcoves, giving visitors privacy as they study various works.

FACING PAGE TOP LEFT & BOTTOM: An 18-karat gold eagle ring by Haida master carver Jim Hart is an excellent example of contemporary jewelry. Jay Simeon is a younger Haida artist who has studied design under Robert Davidson's guidance. One of the finest Haida jewelers working today, Simeon's *Octopus Bracelet* illustrates his craftsmanship.

FACING PAGE TOP RIGHT: World-renowned Haida artist Bill Reid engraved delicate silver earrings in the 1960s. There is a similar pair in the collection of the University of British Columbia's Museum of Anthropology. Reid gained early notoriety for his exceptional work in silver and gold and has become Canada's most famous native artist with his artwork on the Canadian 20-dollar bill. *Photographs by John Calhoun*

"Even the smallest details can make a huge impact in a piece of furniture."

—Michael Trayler

ABOVE: An excellent woodworking teacher in high school piqued my interest in the craft. In 1983, my dream of owning a company became a reality. I absolutely love that I get to design and build pieces of furniture, like the oak dining table and buffet. The table's bookmatched top expands with one or two leaves, and the slightly triangular-shaped base is reflected in the buffet's doorframes. The buffet would typically have one drawer and one shelf, but as with all of our furniture, it is built to order.

FACING PAGE: Since only one craftsman builds each furniture piece from start to finish, that person can pay close attention to detail. For example, the starburst top on the macassar ebony coffee table wraps around the sides and down the legs of the table. Another detail, to which we pay particular attention, is the comfort of our chairs. We build multiple prototypes of a new design to ensure the most comfortable option is achieved. Most sofas and lounge chairs come standard with down-back cushions, and we often build a chair to fit a particular body shape or height.
Photographs by Raeff Miles Photography

> "Well-made hardware will feel like a piece of jewelry in your hand."
>
> —Michael Trayler

ABOVE: Early in my career, I quickly learned the importance—the necessity, even—of being fastidious about materials and hardware. I developed the secretary with a condo home office in mind. Using gorgeous wood to create a functional piece of furniture, I intended to capitalize efficiency in a small space. English brown oak is left to its natural grain and color. It pairs nicely with a bronzed metal base. Inside are drawers, shelving, and a drop-down, leather-insert writing desk, all of which can be customized. The piece also features high-quality hardware; fine furniture should not use standard kitchen hinges. In every project, we strive to use sustainable materials, low-emission adhesives, and virtually waste- and vapor-free stain.

FACING PAGE: Armoires are versatile. The natural beauty of light ash wood made this armoire a spectacular piece. I had a cast bronze handle made to reproduce the ripples in the ocean. My intention was to further connect the piece to nature. I am always pleasantly surprised at how inspiring each log can be. That's one reason I prefer clear finishes to allow the wood color and grain to show.
Photographs by Raeff Miles Photography

"Finish is as important as construction. And if it's not done properly, the entire piece loses value."

—Michael Trayler

RIGHT: A homeowner came to me with a photo of a great room he wanted in his home. I took his ideas, analyzed the space, and created a design that was driven by the two-story vaulted ceiling and appliance locations. Nearly two years later, we finished the enormous project. The traditional white-glazed cabinets are very tall, in keeping with the scale of the room. Glass cabinets add a wonderful focal point on one end of the kitchen. We use only the best hardware, drawer slides, and solid wood materials. The mahogany ceiling is very complex with many details and intricacies. Through good design, a work of art was created.
Photographs by Michael Trayler Designs

FACING PAGE: Designs often come from random inspiration and hours of trial and error. One day, I came into my office and found a pile of veneer strips left on my drawing board. I began playing and ended up creating an interesting woven pattern. After process testing, we created a few new pieces of furniture, including a walnut bed with a large weave and a similarly styled, smaller-weave dining chair.
Photograph by Raeff Miles Photography

SUBLIME INTERIORS

Vancouver, British Columbia

"The design process garners influence from personal history and a psychological affinity toward flow and color within a space."

—Geele Soroka

ABOVE & FACING PAGE: For as long as I can recall, I've had an affinity toward the idea of re-imagined spaces. A natural inclination toward design began as early as my teenage years when I converted an adjacent, smaller bedroom into my very first walk-in closet. In terms of interior design, I have always sought to incorporate one guiding principle within my work: allow form to follow function. This principle influences my approach to projects today, allowing me to bring exceptional design ideas to fruition. When presented with the unique coastal loft-like project, I clearly felt the homeowner would benefit from a natural, serene flow throughout the open space in the heart of the city. Comfort and relaxation were of great importance, as was the need to bring the outdoors inside with plenty of warmth and neutrality for a welcoming ambience. Carefully interspersed circular accents nestled among masculine elements provided a calm sense of balance.

Photographs by Ivan Hunter Photography

"Monochromatic colors can provide an essential feeling of unity within a cohesive space."

—Geele Soroka

LEFT: Dark tones can sometimes make a space feel small; when used correctly, darker tones can actually work beautifully with the lighter elements and help create contrast. Highlighted with ambient lighting—which provides both a sense of relaxation and drama—a sultry grey hue enhances the central column, a stunning structural aspect of the overall layout. I used its unique texture to add visual interest while bringing an element of the surrounding rugged coastal mountains indoors. The smooth concrete ceiling is both softened and complemented by a single-tone silk carpet and textured wallpaper. The adjacent balcony's furnishings feature similar supple leather pieces as used in the living room, again crafting a feeling of natural flow and connection between the inside and out.
Photograph by Ivan Hunter Photography

"When thoughtfully utilized, a specific degree of contrast can create a perfectly balanced space."

—Geele Soroka

TOP LEFT: A solid glass coffee table anchors several sleek leather swivel chairs in the living room and enhances the overall feeling of openness and flow. Every seat offers a stunning view of the gorgeous outdoor setting, while the furniture's rounded edges speak to the seaside context, conjuring up an image of rocks that have been smoothed by the waves.

LEFT: Backlit mirrors provide superior functional lighting for personal grooming and add a feeling of warmth to the small space, while clean lines and other elements of design help create a sophisticated atmosphere.

FACING PAGE: Adjacent to the master bedroom and separated by a discreet, opaque sliding glass door lies the office, a welcome reprieve for the owner. Warm tones of the hardwood floor balance the slightly cooler, darker tones and accents elsewhere. Given the West Coast location and seaside feel, a subtle nautical undertone tastefully punctuates elements of the master bedroom, like the unique bedside lamps playing off the dramatic white sails of nearby Canada Place.

Photographs by Ivan Hunter Photography

TOM BAKKER DESIGN

Surrey, British Columbia

"Just like a painting hung straight maintains a sense of balance in a space, so every aspect of a home must harmoniously blend to create a pleasing, comfortable ambience."

—Tom Bakker

ABOVE: Design must be intentional. Even something as minor as a light switch needs to be positioned correctly, taking both ergonomics and functionality into account. I love challenges. The kitchen has a structural column in the middle. I was told it couldn't be removed, so I added a second column and designed a cabinet with two popup TVs in between. Besides accommodating audio visual components, it also visually divides the kitchen from the sitting room while maintaining spatial openness.

FACING PAGE: The homeowners wanted a grand yet intimate ambience. The footprint is large, which allowed me to design two oversized islands that each have a lot of storage space. The larger island forms a natural transition between the kitchen and the breakfast area. One side of the island accommodates nine large drawers to service breakfast dining, while the smaller island accommodates barstools so guests can be a part of the action. Leaded glass—another design element the homeowners had dreamed about—was elegantly integrated into the upper cabinets.
Photographs by Stephen Cridland

"A positive emotional response at the end of a project is the greatest reward."

—Tom Bakker

ABOVE: Indoor/outdoor living is important to the family, so I replaced three windows in the kitchen with a folding glass door, allowing access to a spectacular deck; they love it. I also wanted to ensure that daylight will continue to filter into the basement, so I collaborated with a glazing and structural engineer to creatively integrate two opaque glass panels into the deck.
Photograph by Stephen Cridland

FACING PAGE TOP: Symmetry and balance make the kitchen feel comfortable and harmonious while intimately enveloping its large square footage. Luxurious details—like the hammered-copper farmer's sink, leaded-glass cabinet fronts, and two-tone interior—add interest to the magnificent award-winning kitchen.
Photograph by Dominic Schaefer

FACING PAGE BOTTOM: Five levels of decking ease guests down the nearly six feet of height difference between the kitchen and the existing grade. I created each level to provide space for a specific function, from dining and lounging to relaxing in the hot tub or mingling in the open space below during parties.
Photograph by Stephen Cridland

"Every project is like a journey, and the entire process should be enjoyed and savored."

—Tom Bakker

TOP: Working with the owners of a beautiful 90-foot motor yacht gave me the opportunity and privilege to create something spectacular. The owners provided many examples of elements they wanted to implement, one of which was the triple oval portholes that I incorporated into their master stateroom.
Photograph courtesy of owner

MIDDLE & BOTTOM: The highly customized floorplan of the galley and dining lounge includes a partial wall featuring an exclusive work of art that I created. The owners wanted to utilize granite throughout, so a specialty fabricator was contracted to reduce the stone slab's thickness to accommodate the weight limits of the vessel. Other details such as fluted columns, triple-crown mouldings, and highly detailed countertop edges coordinate in a well-balanced manner.
Photographs by Onne van der Wal

FACING PAGE: Everything on the yacht was executed to the highest standards possible, from the enclosed aft deck to the mirrored ceiling and curved mouldings to the custom furniture and high-gloss drum table in the salon.
Photograph by Onne van der Wal

WESTCOAST AUDIO VIDEO GALLERY

Vancouver, British Columbia

"Today's electronics don't have to overpower the living space."

—Robert Autar

ABOVE: Good design is crucial in a home, and technology should not be excluded from that concept. With every project, we take our eye for contemporary style and marry it with absolute function, installing only the most advanced equipment. Every home is different, so our team—founder Robert Autar, manager and client consultant Armand Rajkumar, and head of installation and design Morgan McMillan—extensively studies the space, determines what the needs are, and designs a customized system, as we did in the sleek environment where a white television and Leon integrated speaker blend perfectly with the surroundings.

FACING PAGE: In an elegant living area, a beautiful Leon speaker was designed to fit above the television so that it virtually melts into the frame. In addition, we designed an entire electronic control system so the homeowners can adjust the lighting, blinds, audio, video, air conditioning and heating, and security system with just a touch of a button. Often, we create specific scenes for the homeowners, so that one button will adjust all of the elements for a certain function, like entertaining or sleeping.
Photographs by Leon Speakers

"For most people, the look of their audio video system and how it fits in with their total environment is as important as how it sounds and functions."

—Armand Rajkumar

ABOVE: A floorstanding Paradigm speaker looks beautiful with its high-gloss black finish. Surrounded by oversized furniture and a large fireplace, the speakers exude an ornamental feel.

FACING PAGE TOP: For a contemporary theater space that featured warm tones and an intimate feel, we brought in a handmade, high-quality Italian pair of speakers customized with a wood facade. A DreamVision projector, which is very reliable and has good longevity, blends in perfectly with the high-end system. As a finishing touch, the wall is covered with a special paint designed to accept images from the projector.

FACING PAGE BOTTOM: We like to say that we are where high performance meets high style, and our technicians play a huge role in making it happen. Each technician has at least 10 years of experience—not to mention a formal education—but the most important qualities are attention to detail and respect for the homeowner. They are indeed master craftsmen who treat each installation as if it were in their own home, bringing a neatness and perfection to the project that is simply unmatched. Along with a 65-inch panel TV, we recessed Paradigm speakers into the wall for a clean, theater-like ambience.
Photographs by Westcoast Audio Video Gallery

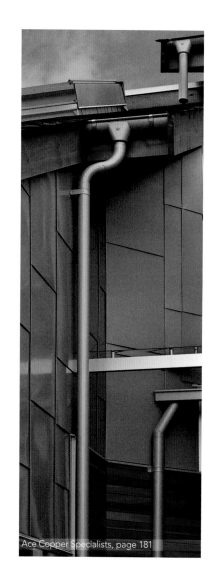

Ace Copper Specialists, page 181

Ace Copper Specialists, page 181

living the elements

Houston Landscapes, page 189

Unison Windows & Doors, page 195

Relkie Art Glass, page 201

Surrey, British Columbia

"There are so many different kinds of metal and each has its own unique personality. The possibilities and complexities are absolutely invigorating."

—Paul Dore

ABOVE & FACING PAGE: Intuitively knowing how the material will behave—how it needs to be worked, treated, installed, and maintained—is what allows us to be confident in the engineering, the aesthetic, and the long-term durability of all of our projects. Architect Dan White came to us with a concept of a hyperbolic metal roof that curves both ways. After many cycles of development, reconfiguration, and mockups, we gridded out the plan and painstakingly produced each 15-inch shingle by hand as the curve needed to be slightly different with each piece. We worked from the low corners to the high point, one row at a time, to ensure that the seams were a perfect match; the artful, flat-lock bronze roof reads as one continuous, mysterious plane. The bronze trellis and accent walls further the sculpted effect and the architecture's connectivity to the site.
Photographs by Dan Stone

"The fact that we've worked on everything from traditional and contemporary homes to a log cabin, a Buddhist temple, waterfalls, and tree sculptures proves just how universal the medium of metal really is."

—Debbie Dore

LEFT: Half-round, European-style gutters are far superior to what is commonly used in Canada because there is less resistance for the water and minimal debris buildup. We went with zinc gutters and side panels for a Vancouver home because of the functionality as well as the distinctly modern look.

FACING PAGE: Metal actually sweats, so ventilation is an absolute requirement. Behind the stainless steel panels of the contemporary home are cavities that promote air flow, promoting proper temperature and humidity regulation. To keep with the clean lines of the roofline, we concealed the gutters and strategically placed the downspouts. I love the way the metal detailing around the house frames the architecture and connects it to the natural setting.
Photographs by Dan Stone

"Just because something hasn't been done before doesn't mean it can't be done."

—Paul Dore

ABOVE & FACING PAGE: Built into the side of a cliff, the house is accessed via an elevator from the garage above, so the copper roof is uniquely visible from multiple vantage points. Because of the roof's prominence, we chose a flat-lock wedge system, which means that rather than capping the copper rib connections, we lapped the seams, fully celebrating both construction method and materiality. The deep overhangs negated the need for gutters, so the look is nice and clean. While the roof and wall panels have a brilliant patina, we can only take credit for insisting that the homeowner allow Mother Nature to work her magic over the course of a few years, rather than forcing a look through chemical treatments.
Photographs by Dan Stone

"The ability to blend old-school ingenuity with the latest technology opens up a world of possibilities to artisans of all varieties."

—Debbie Dore

LEFT & FACING PAGE: Though the home was designed by architect Dan White and the metalwork was designed and executed by our team, the cross-discipline collaboration is evident in the seamless way the metal meets other materials like wood and glass. Rather than competing for attention, all of the elements—large and small—are structurally and visually purposeful. We love how the tree pierces the hyperbolic metal roof to marry the manmade and natural landscapes.

Photographs by Dan Stone

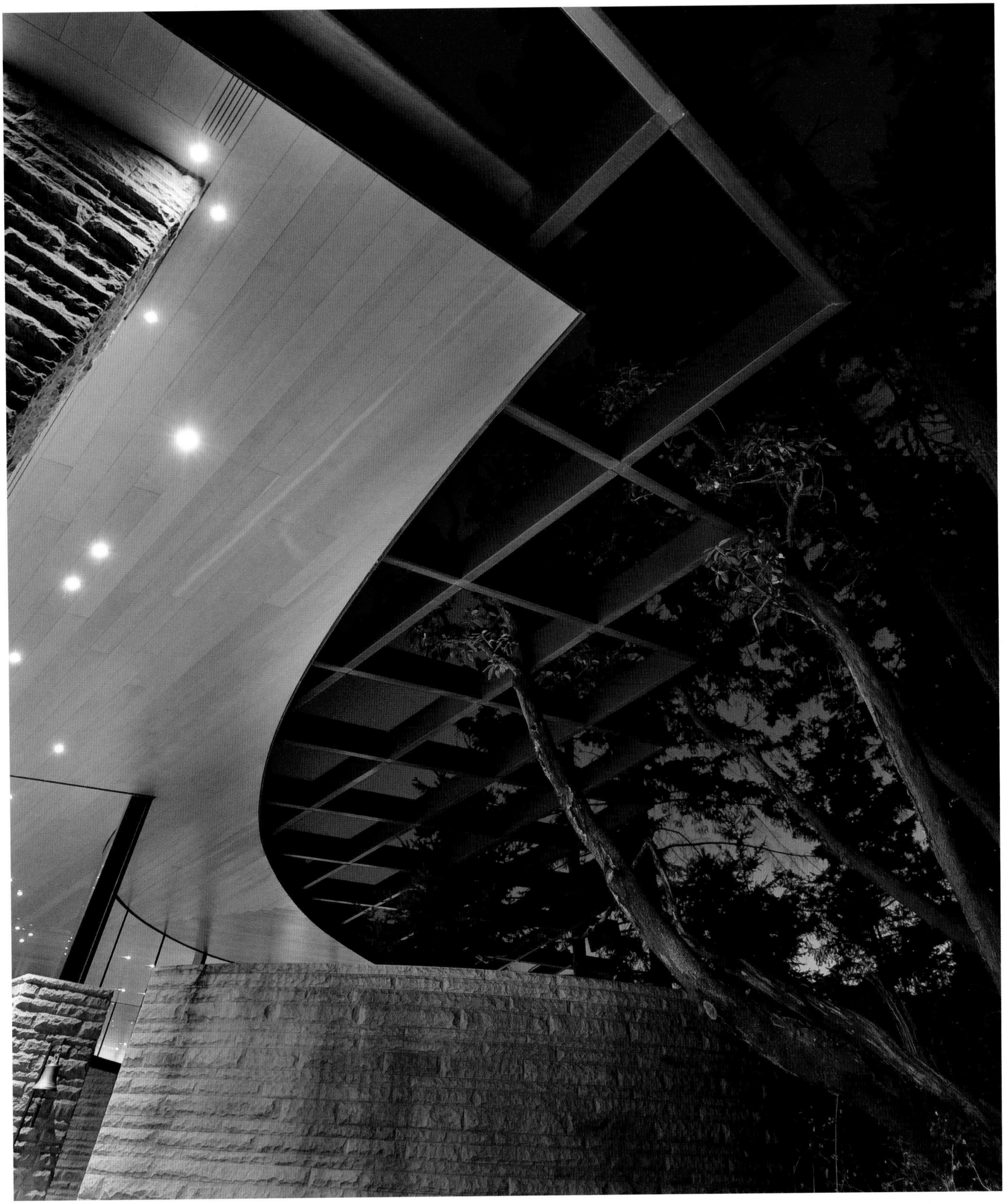

"We believe in being the change we want to see in the world, so sustainability is important in every project."

—Jeremy Miller

ABOVE: The style and atmosphere of the home is our starting point because the outdoor spaces need to be integrated with the rest of the property. For a new construction with a decidedly contemporary feel, we utilized sleek finishes and clean lines through smooth concrete patio and modern furnishings. In the backyard, a slightly casual feel was created with weeping plants and the organic, dry-stack basalt wall.

FACING PAGE: Featuring expansive views from Vancouver Island to Mount Baker, the home exudes contemporary style through architectural concrete walls and structured garden design. We also included a small water feature, a manicured lawn, and a vanishing edge pool.
Photographs by Andrea Sirois

"A good contractor needs to be flexible enough to accommodate preferences but strong enough to guide away from bad decisions."

—Jeremy Miller

ABOVE: Plant selection is crucial, especially in a climate where about eight months of the year provide pleasant weather to enjoy the outdoors. The front bed of the property showcases unique plants that the homeowner loves, such as corkscrew hazelnut and contorted dwarf maple. We used numerous perennials that would provide a variety of color and blooms from spring to fall.

ABOVE RIGHT: Set amidst the lush landscape, we created an outdoor lounging area, which includes a built-in fireplace. The wood deck and matching furniture help break up the stone materials and create a warm atmosphere that blends well with the natural surroundings.

FACING PAGE: We designed a water feature to offer both an audio and visual element to a dark corner of the backyard. Shelves were built into the pond to allow the fish seclusion against predators and provide locations for lighting to highlight the stonework at night.
Photographs by Andrea Sirois

"Transforming a beat-up yard into the nicest one on the street is so rewarding, especially when the homeowner is beaming with pride."

—Jeremy Miller

ABOVE: During a project to transform the backyard of an estate property in West Vancouver, we began with an extensive excavation followed by construction of seven-foot engineered architectural concrete walls. We then installed a 3,000-square-foot dimensional cut basalt pool deck and patio and a vanishing edge swimming pool, which we centered in the large window that acts as a reflective surface from outside.

FACING PAGE: We also completely revamped the entire garden and lawn areas, constructed a cedar fence and pergola, and installed a fireplace, two large firebowls, an audio system, and a waterfall shower. The expansive space features multiple levels and areas to accommodate a variety of activities in all seasons, from dining and lounging to cooking and recreation; it's really all about taking life outside.

Photographs by Andrea Sirois

UNISON WINDOWS & DOORS

North Vancouver, British Columbia

"Well beyond function alone, windows and doors are an essential part of a building's envelope and can be the very key to its character."

—Jim Eisenhauer

ABOVE: This was a simple, unique, and very effective solution. With a combination of long, dramatic lines and natural Douglas fir, it was important that nothing compromise the clean, linear aesthetics of the window wall. Normally installed roll-down shades would have looked like a distracting afterthought, an interruption to the visual flow. Instead, to make everything look "of a piece," we extended the window's jamb out beyond normal depth, running the entire length of the wall. This allowed the shades to fit naturally within the window design and appear to be an actual part of the structure itself.

FACING PAGE: Some simple-looking designs can still present challenges. Here, a custom rake window system with a mix of angles and glass-to-glass corners, all rising cleanly to the ceiling, called for our experience and precision engineering. Our use of the finest European machinery helps us meet the most exacting millwork specs and fit windows like these seamlessly into openings of all shapes and sizes.
Photographs by Andrew Pershin

ABOVE: Bi-fold doors on an ordinary scale are an ordinary job; bi-fold doors on a grand scale demand extraordinary precision and a robust, reliable hardware system. That's how we achieved the massive, 200-square-foot openings that unite the expansive indoor and outdoor living spaces and allow each 10-foot-high door to operate with just a touch of a finger. We gave this home more than 60 linear feet of bi-folding doors.
Photograph by Allan Peters

RIGHT: Using one of our engineered products, we realized the architect's vision in the home for a consistent look between flooring and beams. Our product team has worked with our German partners to develop an ultra-stable, engineered millwork system. This split-species solution combines ideal exterior and interior woods in casings, mouldings, and trims for enhanced durability against outside elements, yet with a greater range of decorative wood choices inside. Working closely with lumber suppliers, we further ensured that all doors have a consistent grain and uniform color.
Photograph by Andrew Pershin

FACING PAGE: Our glass-to-glass corner windows do away with conventional obstructions and free up sightlines, letting views and light pour in.
Photographs by Andrew Pershin

"From every standpoint, wood far outpaces its alternatives. The beauty and long-term economy are definitely superior and nothing has a lower carbon footprint. In the right professional hands and crafted with proper methods, wood products are capable of lasting a lifetime."

—Jim Eisenhauer

ABOVE: British Columbia has some of the highest-grade Douglas fir in the world, giving a home windows and doors of exceptional quality. Despite its large expanse, we created the seamless window wall system completely from natural Douglas fir to perfectly frame the home's lush, green surroundings.
Photograph courtesy of John Michael Hall Corporation

ABOVE RIGHT: For an exclusive condominium complex, we custom-engineered and manufactured these outsized yet smooth-sliding wall sections. Conceived by Weinstein Architects and Urban Designers, the wall integrates existing structural posts into the design for both function and aesthetics; robust German hardware provides feather-light operation.
Photograph courtesy of Sunforest Construction

FACING PAGE: Wood is a natural product and its growth is affected by all kinds of forces: soil conditions, minerals, weather, drying process, and age, to name a few. These elements together create a distinct, individual array of beautiful color tones that simply cannot be recreated in composite materials like vinyl or aluminum. Even in the most modern settings, it's still wood that connects us best with our natural world. We source every piece we use from sustainably managed forests—from native Douglas fir to more exotic types like black walnut or ipê to modified woods like Accoya. We know that it's not just our business, it's our future.
Photograph by Andrew Pershin

"Every home should include something extraordinary that causes people to stop in amazement."

—Neil Relkie

ABOVE: The foyer and living room were essentially one large room, so we added an artistic glass wall and window panel to establish division without removing the spacious feel. The finger-friendly broken edge of the three-dimensional carved glass takes cues from the surrounding rocky landscape, imparting a bit of drama against the home's clean lines.

FACING PAGE: Many people choose to live on the West Coast because of the area's natural beauty and abundant wildlife, so we often reflect the scenery in glasswork. In a home on the Strait of Georgia, we mimicked the dolphins often seen in the bay, continuing their curves into the rounded graphic border.
Photographs by Lance Sullivan

"Glass is more than just something to see through; it's something to admire and study."

—Neil Relkie

LEFT: Using the homeowners' photos of bears as a guide, we created a striking stained glass entry. Not only beautiful, the windows and doors are made as thermal sealed units of tempered safety glass to meet building and safety codes.
Photograph by Team Husar Wildlife Photography

FACING PAGE LEFT: The colorful mermaid scene adds spectacular vibrancy to the house, and the clear textured glass simultaneously allows privacy and fills the foyer with light. The intricate detail of a cougar amidst nature creates a fascinating reflection through the sandblasted glass at night.
Photographs by Lance Sullivan

FACING PAGE RIGHT: The details of the eagle's feathers, talons, and beak showcase the powerful imagery of the carved glass entrance.
Photograph by Lance Sullivan

perspectives
ON DESIGN

WESTERN CANADA TEAM
ASSOCIATE PUBLISHER: Lisa Bridge
GRAPHIC DESIGNER: Paul Strength
EDITOR: Jennifer Nelson
MANAGING PRODUCTION COORDINATOR: Kristy Randall
TRAFFIC SUPERVISOR: Drea Williams

HEADQUARTERS TEAM
PUBLISHER: Brian G. Carabet
PUBLISHER: John A. Shand
SENIOR GRAPHIC DESIGNER: Emily A. Kattan
GRAPHIC DESIGNER: Lilian Oliveira
MANAGING EDITOR: Rosalie Z. Wilson
EDITOR: Alicia Berger
EDITOR: Sarah Tangney
PRODUCTION COORDINATOR: London Nielsen
PROJECT COORDINATOR: Jessica Adams
ADMINISTRATIVE COORDINATOR: Amanda Mathers
CLIENT SUPPORT COORDINATOR: Kelly Traina
ADMINISTRATIVE ASSISTANT: Tommie Runner

PANACHE PARTNERS, LLC
CORPORATE HEADQUARTERS
1424 GABLES COURT
PLANO, TX 75075
469.246.6060
WWW.PANACHE.COM

index

THE PANACHE COLLECTION

CREATING SPECTACULAR PUBLICATIONS FOR DISCERNING READERS

Dream Homes Series
An Exclusive Showcase of the
Finest Architects, Designers and Builders

Carolinas
Chicago
Coastal California
Colorado
Deserts
Florida
Georgia
Los Angeles
Metro New York
Michigan
Minnesota
New England

New Jersey
Northern California
Ohio & Pennsylvania
Pacific Northwest
Philadelphia
South Florida
Southwest
Tennessee
Texas
Washington, D.C.

Spectacular Homes Series
An Exclusive Showcase of the Finest Interior Designers

California
Carolinas
Chicago
Colorado
Florida
Georgia
Heartland
London
Michigan
Minnesota
New England

Metro New York
Ohio & Pennsylvania
Pacific Northwest
Philadelphia
South Florida
Southwest
Tennessee
Texas
Toronto
Washington, D.C.
Western Canada

Perspectives on Design Series
Design Philosophies Expressed
by Leading Professionals

California
Carolinas
Chicago
Colorado
Florida
Georgia
Great Lakes
London

Minnesota
New England
New York
Pacific Northwest
South Florida
Southwest
Western Canada

Art of Celebration Series
Inspiration and Ideas from
Top Event Professionals

Chicago & the Greater Midwest
Colorado
Georgia
New England
New York
Northern California
South Florida
Southern California
Southern Style
Southwest
Toronto
Washington, D.C.

City by Design Series
An Architectural Perspective

Atlanta
Charlotte
Chicago
Dallas
Denver
Orlando
Phoenix
San Francisco
Texas

Spectacular Wineries Series
A Captivating Tour of Established,
Estate and Boutique Wineries

California's Central Coast
Napa Valley
New York
Sonoma County
Texas
Washington

Experience Series
The Most Interesting Attractions,
Hotels, Restaurants, and Shops

Boston
British Columbia
Chicago
Southern California
Twin Cities

Interiors Series
Leading Designers Reveal Their Most Brilliant Spaces

Florida
New York
Southeast

Spectacular Golf Series
An Exclusive Collection of Great Golf Holes

Colorado
Texas
Western Canada

Specialty Titles
The Finest in Unique Luxury Lifestyle Publications

21st Century Homes
Cloth and Culture: Couture Creations of Ruth E. Funk
Distinguished Inns of North America
Extraordinary Homes California
Geoffrey Bradfield Ex Arte
Into the Earth: A Wine Cave Renaissance
Shades of Green Tennessee
Spectacular Hotels
Spectacular Restaurants of Texas
Visions of Design
Southern California Weddings

Panache Books App
Inspiration at Your Fingertips

Download the Panache
Books app in the iTunes
Store to access select
Panache Partners
publications. Each book
offers inspiration at your
fingertips.

Panache Partners, LLC   1424 Gables Court   Plano, Texas 75075   469.246.6060   www.panache.com